Hawksbill Promise

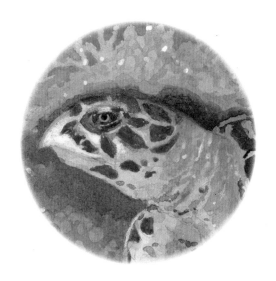

Written and Illustrated by
Mary Beth Owens

Tilbury House Publishers
Thomaston, Maine

For Pam, the Joyfuls, and sister Hawksbill.
—MBO

Tilbury House Publishers
12 Starr Street
Thomaston, Maine 04861
www.tilburyhouse.com

Text and Illustrations © 2019 by Mary Beth Owens

Hardcover ISBN 978-0-88448-430-1
eBook ISBN 978-0-88448-429-5

First hardcover printing May 2019

15 16 17 18 19 20 XXX 10 9 8 7 6 5 4 3 2 1

Library of Congress Control Number: 2019936108

Designed by Kathy Squires in memory of her mom, Dorothy Squires, 11|12|22–02|23|19.

Printed in China through Four Colour Print Group

The illustrations were executed with WN watercolors, acrylics and ink on Arches 300 hot press paper.

Promise

A promise in my DNA

compels me to return one day

to white sands here on Jumby Bay

where I will lay,

will lay,

and lay

a hundred moonlit eggs

so they

may hatch

and scramble out to sea

one day

returning

just like me.

Hawksbill Promise

Written and Illustrated by
Mary Beth Owens

Tilbury House Publishers
Thomaston, Maine

The bright Caribbean sun
beats down on Jumby Bay.
Morning glories run wild
along the beach,
their petals closing as the air
grows hotter.

In the shade
of the sea grape branches
are fallen dry leaves
with the colors
of a turtle's shell.

There is something special
in the sand beneath the leaves,
something only I can see,
and only I can see beneath the surface
of the water over the coral reef
that surrounds my island.

I am the Jumby tree.
I keep watch at the water's edge.
My branches twist and sway,
rising to the sky,
moving to the heartbeat
of the land
and sea.

My roots hold stories
from other islands and continents,
stories that ripple across coral reefs,
echo in sea caves
and off ledges,
drift with the currents,
and murmur over the water's surface.

I carry within me stories of sea turtles
like the one I see waiting in the water
over the coral reef,
gathering strength
for what she will do tonight.

She has swum hundreds of miles
to reach this place,
where she was born
twenty years ago.
She has returned
as surely as a promise.

A soft golden glow
spreads slowly over the island.
Purple clouds in the shape of sea turtles
move across the sky,
foretelling an arrival—
if you have eyes to see.

Her name is Hawksbill,
and I am eager to meet her again!
Come and wait with me.

Darkness surrounds the island
for a long time before
the full moon appears
like a bright fire on the horizon.

Keep watch with me
as I whisper ghost stories
to scare off poachers—
dark, heart-pounding ghost stories
that ripple across the water,
warning those who would hunt
Hawksbill for her beautiful shell.

Who would be afraid of me?
I am only a Jumby tree,
waiting and watching
in the black, inky night.

BOO!

The shadows on the shore loom large,
but the full moon lights a sparkling path
for Hawksbill.

She follows,
heaving herself from the water,
lumbering slowly over the sand,
up the dune,
and under the sea grape leaves.
I whisper a welcome.

Hush now.
Even in the quiet night
I must listen carefully
to hear where Hawksbill
is working.

Tangled roots and thick leaves
on low-hanging branches
form a cover
for her labor.

She has picked a spot.
Her hind flippers take turns,
scooping sand and tossing it aside
to form a deep, soft nest.

The sand receives her eggs.
One after another
they glisten—
a hundred full moons,
round and smooth.

Tears from her eyes
release salt from a thousand dives.
Her shell, brilliant in the water,
looks dull and weathered on land.
It is scratched with graffiti
from the coral reefs where she feeds,
and it is etched with brutal stories—
struck by propeller blades,
gouged by shark jaws,
scored by trawl lines, nets, and hooks.

Her brothers and sisters
did not escape the dangers
marked on her shell.
They will never return
to this place where they hatched.

The sea air
is calling Hawksbill back
to the water.

Shh....
See how she covers
the eggs with sand,
tamps down the surface,
and with all four flippers
flings sand, twigs, and shells,
disguising the nest
she dug so carefully,
doing her best to keep it
safe from intruders.

Her treasure hidden,
she turns slowly
and pushes her heavy body
back over the sand dune,
past roots and branches,
returning to the water,
weightless.

As she dives,
a memory surfaces.
She was once a hatchling,
swirling and drifting
in a mass of golden sargassum.
Sheltered in the floating seaweed,
she stayed close
to the surface of the vast ocean.
Below her waited the shimmering scales
and sharp teeth of hungry fish.

Years passed before she
dove deeper,
found reefs in other oceans,
and, in season, mated with
another hawksbill.

Carrying eggs inside her,
she returned to this coral reef
to lay them on the sandy island
where she was born.

Keep watch with me.
Nights go by.
Hawksbill crawls ashore
three more times
to make nests of eggs.
Then she swims away
to distant waters,
her labor done for now.
For two years, three, or four,
I will wait for her return.
Will you wait with me?

Days pass, then weeks.
Ghost crabs skitter across
the dry sea grape leaves
trying to dig for Hawksbill's eggs.
I sing to those eggs
the ocean's lullaby.
Neither ghost crabs nor mongoose
nor other animals disturb them.

Count the time with me.
One month passes.
Two months.
Then early one morning,
before sunrise,
the first baby turtles hatch.

They thrash and flail
to get free of their shells,
jostling their brothers and sisters.
More eggs hatch!
The nest stirs.

As sand fills in around collapsed egg shells,
dimples appear in the surface above.
The baby turtles rise together,
an eruption of hatchlings!

Up from the sand,
one hundred hatchlings appear.
I count them to be sure.

In the darkness
they look for what
they already know:
the moon, their mother's face;
the starlight, their path;
the wide horizon, their home.

Ready, set...

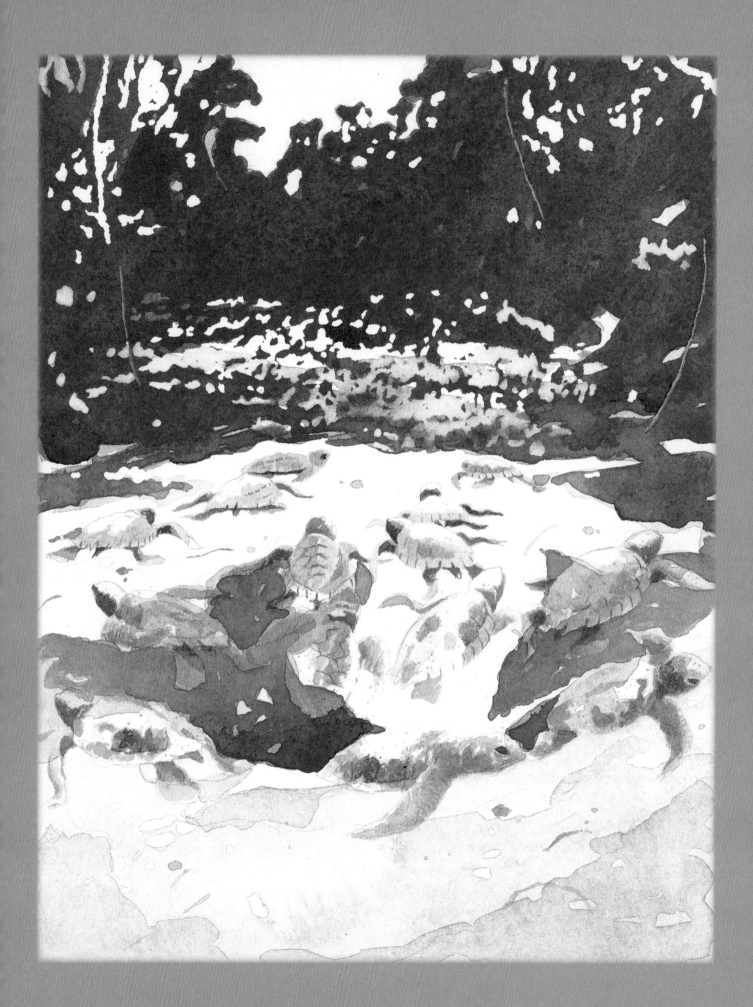

...Go!
First light urges!
Go quickly
past the screeching gulls!
Go bravely
past the hungry herons!

Go safely
over the mighty sand dune!
Go invisibly
through the ghost crabs!
Go to the welcoming sea!

I wait
for the undertow
to carry the hatchlings
into the ocean.

I watch
as they swim away.

Come close
to hear their stories.
I am the Jumby tree.
Come wait.
Keep watch with me.

About Hawksbill

The hawksbill sea turtle *(Eretmochelys imbricata)* is one of the smaller species of sea turtles, typically growing to a shell length of 30 to 37 inches (76 to 94 cm) and a weight of 100 to 150 pounds (45 to 67 kg). The hatchlings are 1 to 2 inches (about 4 cm) long.

The top shell, or *carapace*, is patterned with marbled, radiating streaks of brownish-black on a background of cream, light yellow, honey, amber, orange-red, and rust. The thick scales of the carapace, called *scutes*, overlap to give the shell's rear portion a serrated (sawtooth) outline. The bottom shell, or *plastron*, is clear yellow. The hatchlings are mostly brown.

The hawksbill's flippers have two claws each. The head is elongated and tapers to a point, with a beak-like mouth that gives the turtle its name and allows it to reach into the crevices of coral reefs to find the sponges that are the main component of its diet. Hawksbills also eat sea anemones, shrimp, squid, algae, jellyfish, and the Portuguese man o'war, a venomous hydrozoan whose sting is lethal to many fish.

Hawksbill turtles inhabit the world's tropical oceans. In the Atlantic, they are found throughout the Caribbean Sea and the Gulf of Mexico and along the North and South American coastlines as far north as Virginia and south to Brazil. They are also found in the Indian Ocean and in Western Pacific tropical seas, including the waters of the Philippine Islands and Australia's Great Barrier Reef.

Hawksbill turtles are solitary except when mating, and their life histories are mysterious, though biologists are learning more by tracking hawksbill movements with radio transmitters.

The hatchlings are believed to be *pelagic* (free-swimming) for one to three years after birth, until they get large and tough enough to roam coral reefs and other shallow-water *benthic* (sea bottom) environments where food is plentiful and potential predators are active. The turtles are migratory, roaming widely, but females return to the beaches where they were born (their natal beaches) to make their nests. Caribbean hawksbills reach reproductive age at 10 to 25 years of age, after which females nest every two or three years. They crawl ashore at night in their nesting seasons, making three to six nests at 14- to 16-day intervals, with 100 to 150 eggs in each nest.

It is thought that hawksbill turtle populations have declined approximately 80 percent over the past century or so, and the remaining worldwide population of nesting females is variously estimated at 15,000 to 23,000. The turtles are harvested illegally for their eggs, meat, and especially their shells, which have been widely used since ancient times for tortoiseshell jewelry, combs, eyeglass frames, and inlays in wood boxes, furniture, and musical instruments. The coral reef habitats on which the turtles depend are themselves in decline from ocean acidification, and increased recreational and residential use of nesting beaches has reduced the turtles' nesting habitat. Artificial shore lights can prevent hatchlings from finding their way to the sea. Like other sea turtles, hawksbills are also killed inadvertently by commercial fishing gear and by swallowing plastic bags and other objects that they may mistake for jellyfish.

The hawksbill turtle has been classified as endangered in the U.S. (under the Endangered Species Act) since 1970, and as critically endangered since 1996 by the International Union for Conservation of Nature and Natural Resources. Hawksbills are protected from killing and harassment by the Convention on International Trade in Endangered Species.

Plants and Animals of Jumby Bay

Antigua is a beautiful island with a rich natural history. Many of its animal and plant species are not native but were carried to the islands on the trade winds or currents or were introduced by humans. For example, the Javan mongoose, native to Southeast Asia, was introduced to Caribbean islands in the 1800s to control the rats that were destroying sugarcane crops. Mongoose do kill rats, but they also hunt native birds and eggs, including hawksbill turtle eggs.

The narrator of this book is based on the silk **cotton tree** *(Ceiba petandra)*, also known as a kapok tree. This tree, which grows to 240 feet (73 meters) tall, has spiritual significance in folklore traditions of Antigua and was known as the home of tree spirits. The jumbee or jumby is a spirit of Caribbean folklore that can live in trees and is said to haunt Long Island, the island near the northeast coast of Antigua that is the setting of this story and is also known as Jumby Bay Island.

Sea grapes *(Coccoloba uvifera)* are shrubs with big leathery leaves and fruits that look like grapes and taste good when ripe. Beach morning glory vines *(Ipomoea pescaprae)* have colonized islands throughout the Caribbean; their salt-tolerant seeds are dispersed by ocean currents, and the vines thrive in salty trade-wind air. Sea grapes and beach morning glories have been cultivated to stabilize beach dunes and provide the vegetated habitats that hawksbills prefer for nesting sites.

The following animals, listed alphabetically, appear in the illustrations for this book:

Antilles coqui *(Eleutherodactylus johnstonei)*:
Also known as the Lesser Antillean whistling frog, this common and widespread little amphibian (about 1 inch long) is a creature of fields, gardens, and forests and eats insects and spiders. During mating season, males call to females with a two-note whistle.

Atlantic ghost crab *(Ocypode quadrata)*:
Ranging from Cape Cod to Brazil, these crabs dig burrows in the sand of beach dunes and foreshores and are mostly terrestrial, although they spawn in the sea. They are omnivores, eating clams, insects, plant material, other crabs, and the occasional stray hawksbill hatchling.

Bananaquit *(Cerebra flaveola)*:
These common little finches, usually less than 5 inches (13 cm) long, are also known as sugar birds (perhaps for their habit of stealing sugar from outdoor dining tables). Bananaquits in Antigua have curved bills for obtaining nectar from flowers, and they also eat fruit and insects.

Bluestriped grunt *(Haemulon sciurus)*:
A reef fish.

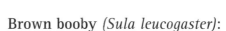

Brown booby *(Sula leucogaster)*:
Like pelicans, these seabirds dive for small fish. Their soaring flights are bookended by bumbling take-offs and landings. Their wingspan can be nearly 5 feet (150 cm), with the females typically growing larger than the males.

Brown pelican *(Pelecanus occidentalis)*: These birds of the tropics, awkward afoot but graceful in flight, can be seen skimming the waves in single file or diving for fish from a height of 70 feet or more.

Caribbean hermit crab *(Coenobita clypeatus)*:
These little animals are land crabs that return to the sea only to lay their eggs. They begin life as plankton, but then metamorphose into tiny versions of their adult selves, emerging from the ocean with borrowed shells serving as their "houses." As they grow, they must search out new shells.

Herring gull *(Larus argentatus)*

Javan mongoose *(Herpestes javanicus)*

Laughing gull *(Larus atricilla)*

Leach's anole *(Anolis leachii)*

Sergeant major fish *(Abudefduf saxatilis)*:
A gregarious reef fish found in shallow waters.

Skink lizard *(Mabuya mabouya)*

Zebra longwing butterfly
(Heliconius charithonia)

Author's Note

Shortly after I agreed to illustrate a picture book about the hawksbill sea turtle, a serendipitous meeting at a campground with a marine biologist just back from tagging female turtles in the Caribbean set the stage for me to observe hawksbills firsthand.

The Jumby Bay Hawksbill Project is the world's longest-running program monitoring hawksbill turtles. I had the extraordinary privilege of shadowing a research team during my visit to the study site at Pasture Bay beach on Long Island, a 300-acre island off the northeast coast of Antigua. Through the quiet night, punctuated with hourly beach patrols, we waited and watched for an egg-bearing female hawksbill to come ashore, and we listened for a turtle that may have slipped past our watchful (or sleepy) eyes to crawl under the sea grapes and begin digging her nest.

From sundown to sunup we waited and watched, and to my astounded delight, we had such a visitation. I was granted a rare opportunity to observe the team collecting data and tagging a turtle, and to immerse my senses in the magical setting as inspiration for Hawksbill Promise.

I hope this book will ignite a curiosity to learn more about hawksbills—about what makes them unique among the world's seven marine turtles, and why they are critically endangered. This book is more an experiential impression of the hawksbill and its habitat than a natural history. The websites listed on the next page offer further information.

In the verse that begins this book, I imagine that the DNA coding of a female hawksbill, which urges her to return to the place of her hatching when it is time to lay her eggs, is like a promise to ensure the continuation of her species. Our gratitude for this requires a response, a promise of our own to ensure that she will always have a beach in which to dig her nest and an ocean in which to thrive.

Further Resources

Books

Florida's Sea Turtles. Victoria B. Van Meter, Florida Power and Light Company, 1992.

Online

Flora & Fauna of Antigua: Trees
www.antiguahistory.net/Museum/fauna.htm#TREES
Background about sea grapes and jumby trees from the Museum of Antigua & Barbuda.

The Guardian
www.theguardian.com/environment/2018/nov/13/hawksbill-turtle-poaching-to-be-fought-with-dna-technology

Jumby Bay Hawksbill Project
www.jbhp.org
This project began in 1987, and turtles that were first tagged back then are still crawling ashore to lay eggs during nesting season.

Wider Caribbean Sea Turtle Conservation Network
www.widecast.org
"Working together to realize a future where all inhabitants of the Wider Caribbean Region, human and sea turtle alike, can live together in balance."

National Oceanic and Atmospheric Administration
https://www.fisheries.noaa.gov/species/hawksbill-turtle

National Wildlife Federation
https://www.nwf.org/Educational-Resources/Wildlife-Guide/Reptiles/
Sea-Turtles/Hawksbill-Sea-Turtle

Our Endangered World
www.ourendangeredworld.com/species/reptiles/hawksbill-sea-turtle

Sea Turtle Conservancy
https://conserveturtles.org/information-about-sea-turtles-hawksbill-sea-turtle

Mary Beth Owens is an award-winning author and illustrator of children's books, among them *Panda Whispers, Counting Cranes,* and *Be Blest: A Celebration of Seasons*. Her book *A Caribou Alphabet* (Tilbury House Publishers) was named an ALA Notable Book and declared a "tour de force" by the *New York Times*. She incorporates her passion for the natural world with her enthusiasm for children's books and teaching art. Research trips have taken her to study caribou in northern Maine, whooping cranes in New Mexico and Texas, sea turtles in Antigua, and marsupials in Australia.